The Great "I AM"
A Study of the Book of Exodus

THE REV. CHARLIE & BROOKE HOLT

© 2023 Bible Study Media, Inc.

All rights reserved.

Published in Jacksonville, Florida by Bible Study Media, Inc.
Cover and Interior design by Shelby Dinkel of Dinkel Digital, LLC.

ISBN # 978-1-942243-67-0
Library of Congress Control Number: 2023914958

No part of this publication may be reproduced, stored in a retrieval system, or transmitted in any form or by any means electronic, mechanical, photocopy, recording, or otherwise except for brief quotations in printed reviews, without the prior written permission of the publisher.
www.biblestudymedia.com.

All Scripture quotations are from the ESV® Bible (The Holy Bible, English Standard Version®), copyright © 2001 by Crossway, a publishing ministry of Good News Publishers. Used by permission.
All rights reserved.

Printed in the United States of America.

Table of Contents

INTRODUCTION	04
WEEK 1: THE GOD WHO KNOWS HIS PEOPLE	06
WEEK 2: THE GOD WHO REDEEMS HIS PEOPLE	10
WEEK 3: THE GOD WHO SAVES HIS PEOPLE	14
WEEK 4: THE GOD WHO HEALS HIS PEOPLE	18
WEEK 5: THE GOD WHO SPEAKS TO HIS PEOPLE	22
WEEK 6: THE GOD WHO DWELLS WITH HIS PEOPLE	26
WEEK 7: THE GOD WHO SANCTIFIES HIS PEOPLE	30
WEEK 8: THE GOD WHO LOVES HIS PEOPLE	34
WEEK 9: THE GOD WHO GUIDES HIS PEOPLE	38
APPENDICES	
FREQUENTLY ASKED QUESTIONS	42
SMALL GROUP COVENANT	44
GROUP CALENDAR	45
PRAYER & PRAISE JOURNAL	46
SMALL GROUP ROSTER	48
SMALL GROUP LEADER HELPS	49
HOSTING AN OPEN HOUSE	49
LEADING FOR THE FIRST TIME	49
LEADERSHIP TRAINING 101	50

Introduction

The Book of Exodus is one of the greatest love stories ever told. God is revealed as Yahweh, the Great "I AM." He is the transcendent, all-powerful creator of all things who defeated the greatest powers of the earth. This same God would have his people know and love him in an intimate and personal way.

Come explore the grand story of God as the one who knows and loves his people. In learning the self-revelation of God, we discover our identity and the abundant life he has for us. God knows the suffering and struggles of his people. The Lord would not only redeem and deliver them but also lead them with his personal presence into becoming his kingdom of priests.

Ultimately, the Exodus story will become our own story as the Great "I AM" visits his people in the person of Jesus Christ who, through his cross and resurrection, brings us through a New Exodus from the spiritual forces of evil, sin, and death.

— Brooke and Charlie Holt+

Using This Study

Studying God's Word is an investment. But with our good God, entrusting him with your time and your heart yields only reward! So give all you can. As you invest in this study, know God will be faithful to you.

To aid in your endeavor, here are some guidelines for you and your group to review before you get started.

How to Get the Most Out of This Study

1. Review the Table of Contents.
2. If you're hosting or facilitating a group, read the section entitled "Small Group Leader Helps." It lays out best practices for how to host or facilitate a healthy small group and avoid common mistakes. It's a great idea to review this material before your first meeting.
3. Adapt this book to the needs of your group. If a line of discussion leads to green pastures outside the scope of the book, enjoy the leading of the Good Shepherd. Feel free to ask, or allow other members to ask, insightful questions as the Holy Spirit leads.
4. Relax and remember you do not have to ask every question in your group discussion. There is a lot of material here. Feel free to skip questions as needed and linger over the ones where there is authentic conversation.
5. Enjoy the experience. Christian community should be characterized by joy and love. Encourage yourself and your group members to bear such fruit.
6. Pray before each session. Ask God to minister to you, the host, the facilitator, and every group member by name. Pray for the discussion, the fellowship, and the personal application.
7. Read the "Outline of Each Session" section so you understand the flow of the session and how the study works.

Outline of Each Session

Question
This opening question sets the tone for the week's study. Read it aloud in your group and encourage members to consider the answer as you move through the study.

Key Verse
Each session begins with a key verse or verses. This passage is central to understanding the entire week's theme. You may want to memorize the key verses. By committing portions of God's Word to long-term memory, you will have them to lean on and hope in even when you don't have a Bible with you.

Session Introduction
This section briefly introduces the subject of the week's video lesson. The subject will also reflect the theme your group has been learning about in the week's daily readings. You may wish to have a group member read this section aloud to the group.

Daily Exodus Reading Plan
Use the suggested daily Scripture passages to guide your personal study throughout the week.

Exodus: Leaving Egypt
Opening Prayer
An opening prayer is included in each session that reflects the session's theme. You may read this aloud to begin your study or have someone in your group lead in an opening prayer.

Getting Started
These opening questions are like "warm-ups" that will explore how you were able to apply the previous week's session and get you started studying this week's lesson.

Sinai: Meeting at the Mountain
Watch the Video
Play the video for your group, making sure the volume is adequate for all to hear and that every member can see the video from where they're sitting. The video teaching resources for The Great "I AM": A Study of the Book of Exodus may be found on the web at: biblestudymedia.com/pages/the-great-i-am/

You can also find them on the Bible Study Media App's Digital Library page in your App Store on your mobile device or on the Bible Study Media App/Channel on Apple TV or Roku.

Video Notes
This section summarizes key points made in the video. If a lot of material has been covered in the teaching, you may want to help briefly "sum it up" for your group with these notes.

Shema: Hearing God's Covenant Word
This section is the reading of God's life-giving and everlasting Word—his goodness to his people. It also includes questions for the application and discussion of the Scripture passage. The more we feed on God's Word and experience his goodness through his Word, the more we will crave him. And, as we partake in God's truths with our community of God's people, we will feast on the fullness of his provision to us.

Tabernacle: Journeying with Glory
This section will focus on what it means to use the spiritual nourishment we have just received as fuel to live lives of service to God and to others.

Prayer Requests
After the group discussion, you have the option of asking members for prayer requests they'd like the group to pray for. There is a Prayer & Praise Journal included in this Study Guide to keep track of prayer requests and God's gracious answers!

Closing Prayer
Close your group's time in prayer, either with someone leading in a summary closing prayer, or provide space for multiple people to pray. Make sure to be mindful of your group's time constraints.

Week 1: THE GOD WHO KNOWS HIS PEOPLE
Exodus 1:1–5:21

QUESTION

The book of Exodus begins with the statement that a new king arose over Egypt, and he did not know Joseph. What is the importance of being known? How is God making himself known?

KEY VERSE

"During those many days the king of Egypt died, and the people of Israel groaned because of their slavery and cried out for help. Their cry for rescue from slavery came up to God. And God heard their groaning, and God remembered his covenant with Abraham, with Isaac, and with Jacob. God saw the people of Israel – and God knew." — Exodus 2:23-25

SESSION INTRODUCTION

For 400 years, the people of Israel were slaves in Egypt. We read of their affliction and groaning. While Pharaoh did not know Joseph, the Lord did. Not only did the Lord remember Joseph, but he remembered his covenantal promises to Abraham, Isaac, and Jacob. Israel was his firstborn son. While Pharaoh did not care for the Israelites, the Lord did care for them. He heard their groaning, he cared about their cries, and he had a plan for their redemption.

To be known is to be loved. *"God saw the people of Israel and God knew"* (2:25). Just as a parent knows his or her child, so God knows his people. In knowing them, he loves them.

To be known is to be understood. *"Their cry for rescue from slavery came up to God"* (2:23). The Lord heard the cries of his children, and he understood their pain. The Lord saw their desperate situation. He knew, he understood, and he cared for his people.

To be known is to be valued. *"And God heard their groaning, and God remembered his covenant with Abraham, Isaac, and Jacob"* (2:24). The Israelites were God's chosen people. They were precious to him, his firstborn son. Because of their great value, the Lord will redeem his people from their slavery. He will fulfill his covenant.

READING PLAN: WEEK ONE

DAY 1	EXODUS 1:1–22
DAY 2	EXODUS 2:1–10
DAY 3	EXODUS 2:11–25
DAY 4	EXODUS 3:1–22
DAY 5	EXODUS 4:1–17
DAY 6	EXODUS 4:18–31
DAY 7	EXODUS 5:1–21

EXODUS: LEAVING EGYPT

Opening Prayer

Lord, you know us. You have always known us, always seen us, and always heard us. You know the deepest cries of our hearts. We thank you for your perfect care for us. Lead us now into a deeper knowing of you, into a deeper relationship with you, and into a deeper trust in your sovereign plan for our lives. In the name of Jesus Christ our Lord we pray, Amen.

Getting Started

1. If this is the first time your group has met or if you have new members, take some time to go around and introduce yourselves. What are your hopes for joining this group and your study of the book of Exodus?

2. The first chapters of Exodus show how the providential working of the Lord will ultimately lead to his plan of salvation for the nation of Israel. How does it comfort you to know that God always has a plan of salvation for his people? Do you believe that he has a plan for your circumstances today?

SINAI: MEETING AT THE MOUNTAIN

Watch the Video

The video teaching resources for The Great "I AM": A Study of the Book of Exodus may be found on the web at: biblestudymedia.com/pages/the-great-i-am/

You can also find them on the Bible Study Media App's Digital Library page in your App Store on your mobile device or on the Bible Study Media App/Channel on Apple TV or Roku.

Video Notes

God knows his people. The book of Exodus begins with the names of the sons of Israel who came to Egypt. A new Pharaoh arose who did not know Joseph, and he was deeply threatened by the strength of the Israelite nation, so he set taskmasters over them and forced them into slavery. The nation of Israel went from being renowned throughout Egypt to being oppressed. While it seemed that their cries and misery were unnoticed and unheard, the Lord saw, heard, and knew all their affliction.

The Lord remembers his covenant. The Lord knows his people, loves his people, and has a plan for their deliverance. In his sovereignty, the Lord has always known the plan for his people. In Genesis 15:13, the Lord makes a covenant with Abraham and speaks these words: *"Know for certain that your offspring will be sojourners in a land that is not theirs and will be servant there, and they will be afflicted for four hundred years."* Even before Joseph was born, the Lord knew his people would be in Egypt. The providential hand of the Lord will be seen all throughout the book of Exodus. He will be working on behalf of his people, working out his plan and purpose in his time.

The Lord loves his children. Throughout the book of Exodus, Yahweh is inviting the nation of Israel to know him. Just as the Pharoah had forgotten Joseph and his history in the land of Egypt, so the Hebrews had forgotten the Lord. When facing their afflictions, the people groaned to their taskmasters and cried out to Pharaoh instead of to the Lord.

Apart from the Lord, we are insecure. When Moses received his call from the Lord, he asked the question, "Who shall I say has sent me?" Graciously, the Lord would remind Moses and the people of his covenants, of his steadfast love, of his attributes, and of who they are to him – his firstborn son. This knowledge would strengthen Moses to the task of leadership.

SHEMA: HEARING GOD'S COVENANT WORD

Read Exodus 3:1-4:13: *The Calling of Moses*

3. Moses went from living in the palace of Pharaoh to living in a tent in the desert wilderness of Midian. He went from all the royal privileges to serving as a shepherd (a detestable occupation to the Egyptian people). How do you think both experiences shaped Moses to be the deliverer of his people? How has God used the experiences in your life to shape you and prepare you for your roles and ministries?

4. After beholding the burning bush and hearing the Lord's call, Moses offered five excuses as to why he was not the person for the job. What excuses of Moses most resonate with you? What do you think God wants you to know about your own insecurities?

Five Excuses:
3:11: Unqualified – who am I?
3:13: Don't have authority over people – who will I say sent me?
4:1: No credibility – what if they don't believe me or listen?
4:10: I am not eloquent – slow of speech.
4:13: Send someone else!

Burning Bush by Sébastien Bourdon

5. Just as Moses made excuses when God called him, so we are prone to highlight our insecurities when God calls us. Thankfully, the Lord's call was not dependent on the character of Moses but on the character of God. How does God overcome Moses' excuses?

6. When sending Moses to lead the Israelites, God reveal his name "I AM WHO I AM" (3:14) – the personal and intimate name for God which we say as Yahweh How does knowing God's name help build confidence for Moses' calling?

TABERNACLE: JOURNEYING WITH GLORY

7. Hebrews 4:15 says, "For we do not have a high priest who is unable to sympathize with our weaknesses, but one who in every respect has been tempted as we are, yet without sin." Jesus took on human flesh so that he could not only know our temptations and tribulations but sympathize with us in them. How does this passage minister to you today?

8. Do you have a sense of God's calling for your life? If not, what could be the first step toward discerning your call?

9. What main learning you will apply to your life this week?

PRAYER REQUESTS

You may want to share prayer requests with one another. There's a Prayer & Praise Journal found on p. 64 where you can keep track of your group's requests. Have someone close in prayer or pray together as a group.

CLOSING PRAYER

Week 2 — THE GOD WHO REDEEMS HIS PEOPLE
Exodus 5:22-9:35

QUESTION
What does it mean to be redeemed by God? How does our redemption change the way we value relationships?

KEY VERSE
"Say therefore to the people of Israel, 'I am the LORD, and I will bring you out from under the burdens of the Egyptians, and I will deliver you from slavery to them, and I will redeem you with an outstretched arm and with great acts of judgment." — Exodus 6:6

SESSION INTRODUCTION

Through the story of the Exodus, we learn new revelations about the nature of God. This week, we will see God revealed as the great redeemer.

The language of redemption comes from the marketplace, particularly the slave market. The Israelites were under the bondage of a cruel slave master who did not want to give up his captives. Their release would be costly.

In the case of the Egyptians, the price would be the death of the firstborn sons of Egypt. For the Israelites, God would redeem them with the blood of the Passover lamb. The angel of death "passed over" the nation of Egypt. Whoever had spread the blood of a sacrificed lamb would receive their freedom, be released from bondage, and be adopted as God's son.

The costly redemption of the Israelites from Egypt pointed to an even greater and more costly redemption. Jesus' death on the cross made the payment to release us from the bondage of sin and death.

READING PLAN: WEEK TWO

DAY 8	EXODUS 5:22–6:13
DAY 9	EXODUS 6:14–30
DAY 10	EXODUS 7:1–13
DAY 11	EXODUS 7:14–25
DAY 12	EXODUS 8:1–15
DAY 13	EXODUS 8:16–9:7
DAY 14	EXODUS 9:8–35

EXODUS: LEAVING EGYPT

Opening Prayer

Lord God, Heavenly Father, you have redeemed us from the bondage of sin and death. Thank you for sending your Son, Jesus Christ to be a perfect sacrifice and atonement for us. Help us to know your love and to see the value that you have placed on our lives as your people. In the name of your Son our Lord, Jesus Christ, Amen.

Getting Started

1. What do people mean when they say, "I need to redeem myself"? What does it mean to be redeemed?

2. Where do you see human beings being de-valued or undervalued in our world today? How can we know that human life matters to God?

SINAI: MEETING AT THE MOUNTAIN

Watch the Video

The video teaching resources for The Great "I AM": A Study of the Book of Exodus may be found on the web at: biblestudymedia.com/pages/the-great-i-am/

You can also find them on the Bible Study Media App's Digital Library page in your App Store on your mobile device or on the Bible Study Media App/Channel on Apple TV or Roku.

The Passover in the Holy Family: Gathering Bitter Herbs by Dante Gabriel Rossetti

Video Notes

Life is valuable. The Israelites had great value to the Pharaoh. But the bottom line is that they did not belong to him—they belonged to Yahweh, the Great "I AM." As Moses said on behalf of Yahweh to Pharaoh, "Let my people go!"

Hardness of heart has consequences. The hardness of Pharaoh's heart to the command of God would result in judgment and wrath for the nation of Egypt. For their rebellion, a series of ten plagues culminating in the Passover would be signs of the mighty arm of Yahweh and mighty acts of his judgement. Ultimately, Pharaoh would lose his firstborn son as a result of refusing to release Yahweh's beloved son (See Exodus 4:22-23).

Jesus brought a New Exodus. God has worked an even greater Exodus in Jesus Christ. Sin is the ultimate and greatest oppressor in our lives. Jesus has redeemed us from the power of sin by the shedding of his blood. By his sacrifice as a Passover lamb of atonement, he liberates us from the cruel bondage of sin in all its forms, in order that we might be delivered from the oppressive powers of Satan and the corrupt powers of the world. Jesus would later redefine the Passover meal to signify his body and blood given as redemption for the forgiveness of sins (See Mark 14:22-24). As the Scriptures teach, *"God so loved the world, that he gave his only Son, that whoever believes in him should not perish but have eternal life"* (John 3:16).

SHEMA: HEARING GOD'S COVENANT WORD

Read Exodus 6:1-13: God Promises Deliverance

3. In Exodus 6:2-9 God acknowledges the difficulties in the relationship he has with his enslaved people. What do you see as the main problem identified in these verses?

4. The phrase "I am the LORD" (Yahweh, "The Great I Am") occurs four times in this part of the story. Why do you think it is so important God repeats the phrase again and again?

5. In the video, Charlie and Brooke spoke about the Passover as the fulfillment of God's promise to redeem his people from slavery. How is Jesus' death on the cross like the Passover (See Romans 3:23-25)? What does it mean that his blood is *"received by faith"*?

6. In Exodus 6:6-8, Yahweh makes a series of at least seven "I will" promises to his people. Make a list of them. Why was it so hard for the Israelites to even listen to these promises (v. 9)?

TABERNACLE: JOURNEYING WITH GLORY

7. The Exodus story describes the Israelites struggling with the tension between the reality of their current suffering and God's promise of future redemption and deliverance. How is your experience like theirs?

8. Read Romans 8:18-27. In these verses, the Apostle Paul describes the creation, our bodies, and even the Holy Spirit as groaning under the burden of slavery and futility as we await the fullness of our redemption. What assurance do you have from these verses that God cares about you during times of struggle?

9. Read 1 Corinthians 5:6-8. What are the implications of "Christ, our Passover, has been sacrificed for us"? How does your Passover redemption change the way you value your relationship with God, your relationship with yourself, and your relationship with others?

10. What is one thing that you will do this week to represent a renewed sense of human value and worth in light of Jesus Christ's act of redemption?

PRAYER REQUESTS

You may want to share prayer requests with one another. There's a Prayer & Praise Journal found on p. 64 where you can keep track of your group's requests. Have someone close in prayer or pray together as a group.

CLOSING PRAYER

Week 3 — THE GOD WHO SAVES HIS PEOPLE
Exodus 10:1-14:20

QUESTION

What does it mean to be saved? How are God's people saved and from what are God's people being saved?

KEY VERSE

"And Moses said to the people, 'Fear not, stand firm, and see the salvation of the LORD, which he will work for you today. For the Egyptians whom you see today, you shall never see again. The LORD will fight for you, and you have only to be silent.'"
— Exodus 14:13-14

SESSION INTRODUCTION

The Great I AM is revealed as a mighty warrior who fights for his people. In the most dramatic action of God other than Jesus' resurrection, the Hebrews were rescued from their cruel bondage and tyrannical enemy. Their persecutor was dealt a fatal blow.

As the Hebrews fled Egypt following the ten plagues culminating in the Passover, they were led into a seemingly impossible situation. On the one side, Pharaoh's chariot army pursued and on the other side stood an impassable barrier. But Yahweh saved his people. As Moses set his staff in the waters, they parted, thus providing the path of deliverance for the Hebrews and setting forth the path of destruction for the Egyptian chariot army.

Anticipating the New Exodus through Jesus, the parting of the sea foreshadows the great salvation wrought through the cross and resurrection. Our baptism into his mighty acts delivers us from the three great powers of evil: Satan, the world, and sin. Through Jesus, we are transferred from the dominion of darkness into the marvelous light of the kingdom of God. One day, our mighty warrior will deliver us from a final enemy, death itself.

READING PLAN: WEEK THREE

DAY 15	EXODUS 10:1-20
DAY 16	EXODUS 10:21-11:10
DAY 17	EXODUS 12:1-20
DAY 18	EXODUS 12:21-39
DAY 19	EXODUS 12:40-51
DAY 20	EXODUS 13:1-22
DAY 21	EXODUS 14:1-20

EXODUS: LEAVING EGYPT

Opening Prayer

Lord, you are a warrior who fights for his people. Thank you for the great salvation that you have given to us in your Son, Jesus Christ. We have been delivered from the powers of evil and darkness and transferred to the kingdom of your Son. Give us joy in the freedom of your grace and power. In Jesus' name we pray, Amen.

Getting Started

1. Briefly share your salvation story.

2. Have you ever had the experience of someone fighting for you? How does that feel?"

SINAI: MEETING AT THE MOUNTAIN

Watch the Video

The video teaching resources for The Great "I AM": A Study of the Book of Exodus may be found on the web at: biblestudymedia.com/pages/the-great-i-am/

You can also find them on the Bible Study Media App's Digital Library page in your App Store on your mobile device or on the Bible Study Media App/Channel on Apple TV or Roku.

Crossing of the Red Sea by Possibly Hans Jordaens III

Video Notes

God gives either salvation or judgment. The dramatic rescues of the Bible always demonstrate both the mercy of God and the justice of God, the blessings and the curses. In the story of Noah's ark, while Noah and his family were saved in the ark, the corrupt population of the world was judged in the overwhelming flood. In the merciful deliverance of the Israelites, their salvation, meant severe judgement for Egypt. In the same way the cross and the resurrection represent a victorious triumph over the spiritual forces of evil.

Seek repentance unto salvation. As Moses was sent as Yahweh's agent of salvation, Jesus came to save his people from their sins—that is the meaning of his name (See Matthew 1:21). Yet, while Yahweh wins the victory, we still must choose by faith to walk in that victory. For the Israelites, it meant walking through the parted waters of the sea. For us, it means turning and walking by faith in the confession of Jesus as Lord. The Scriptures promise that *"if you confess with your mouth that Jesus is Lord and believe in your heart that God raised him from the dead, you will be saved"* (Romans 10:9).

Baptism signifies our salvation. Paul writes in 1 Corinthians 10:1-3: *"For I do not want you to be unaware, brothers, that our fathers were all under the cloud, and all passed through the sea, and all were baptized into Moses in the cloud and in the sea … "* The great deliverance of the Israelites through the waters of the sea was Israel's baptism into their salvation. In the same way our water baptism signifies our salvation and points to the reality of the great victory of Jesus over evil on our behalf. Our warrior has won the battle for us; now we must learn to walk in his victory.

SHEMA: HEARING GOD'S COVENANT WORD

Read Exodus 14:1-31: *Crossing the Red Sea*

3. Even though the people of Israel had seen the power of God in their redemption through the Passover, they still doubted God for their ultimate deliverance from Egypt. What do you observe about the people's response to Moses and the Lord in Exodus 14:10-13? Do you resonate with it? How does the Lord reassure them?

4. Read Exodus 14:15-16. What does the Lord ask Moses? What does he tell him to do? How do you see prayer and faith-filled action working simultaneously?

5. The Egyptians realized that the Lord fights for his people (14:25). How does this knowledge encourage you in your exodus from the tyranny of sin and evil powers (See Hebrews 2:14-15)?

6. Why was this dramatic action on God's part so important for the people of Israel to experience and witness (See Exodus 14:30-31)?

TABERNACLE: JOURNEYING WITH GLORY

7. Just as the people were freed from their slavery in Egypt by passing through the waters of the Red Sea, so we are freed from our spiritual slavery when we pass through the waters of baptism (See 1 Corinthians 10:1-3). Discuss this correlation.

8. In our baptism, we renounce Satan and the spiritual forces of evil that rebel against God, the evil powers of this world which corrupt and destroy the creatures of God, and sinful desires that draw us from the love of God. How does God save us from these powers and forces?

9. God would not only redeem us through the cross, but also deliver us from the bondage of sin and death. How does Paul describe our need for deliverance in Romans 7:18-25?

10. Drawing on the themes of the Exodus, Paul writes: *"He has delivered us from the domain of darkness and transferred us to the kingdom of his beloved Son, in whom we have redemption, the forgiveness of sins"* (Colossians 1:13-14). Do you see yourself as having been saved by Jesus' deliverance and redemption?

11. If not, would you want to call on his name for salvation today?

12. If so, what is a personal action step of faith that you will make this week as one who has been "transferred" from one kingdom to another?

PRAYER REQUESTS

You may want to share prayer requests with one another. There's a Prayer & Praise Journal found on p. 64 where you can keep track of your group's requests. Have someone close in prayer or pray together as a group.

CLOSING PRAYER

Week 4 — THE GOD WHO HEALS HIS PEOPLE
Exodus 15:1-19:15

QUESTION
The Lord continues to reveal his attributes to his people. Here, we learn that God is the Great "I Am" who heals you. How can we experience God's healing in our lives?

KEY VERSE
"If you will diligently listen to the voice of the LORD your God, and do that which is right in his eyes, and give ear to his commandments and keep all his statutes, I will put none of the diseases on you that I put on the Egyptians, for I am the LORD, your healer."
— Exodus 15:26

SESSION INTRODUCTION

God has delivered his people from Egypt. Physically, the Israelites are free from their oppression and slave labor. While it took only a few days for God to deliver them physically, it will take forty years in the wilderness to deliver them spiritually. The Lord desires for his people to live free and abundant lives in him. For the Israelites to live in this freedom, they are going to have to let go of the old before they can embrace the new.

The same can be said of us today. The Lord longs to set us free from the bondage of sin so that we can walk in his abundant life. However, the lure of sin is strong. Like the Israelites, we remember the good foods we used to eat, the good wine we used to drink, the pleasures we enjoyed in our land of bondage. Instead of relentlessly looking forward to the abundant life of Christ, we keep looking back at what we have left behind. Nostalgically, we look back longingly for those things.

Just as the Lord taught the Israelites a new way, he wants to teach us to walk according to his plans and purposes. Israel will learn that God's laws are given for their instruction and protection. When they follow those laws, they experience health and vitality. When they disobey, they experience disease and death. Obedience led to their healing; obedience will lead to our healing as well. In this lesson, we will consider the call to live in alignment with the Lord's laws.

READING PLAN: WEEK FOUR

DAY 22	EXODUS 14:21-31
DAY 23	EXODUS 15:1-27
DAY 24	EXODUS 16:1-12
DAY 25	EXODUS 16:13-26
DAY 26	EXODUS 17:1-16
DAY 27	EXODUS 18:1-27
DAY 28	EXODUS 19:1-25

EXODUS: LEAVING EGYPT

Opening Prayer

Teach us, O Lord, to trust and obey you. Teach us to diligently delight ourselves in your will and way that we may live abundantly in this world and, in the world to come, have everlasting life. In Jesus Christ's name, Amen.

Getting Started

1. Do you believe that God still heals today?

2. Where do you long to see healing in your life, family, or community?

SINAI: MEETING AT THE MOUNTAIN

Watch the Video

The video teaching resources for The Great "I AM": A Study of the Book of Exodus may be found on the web at: biblestudymedia.com/pages/the-great-i-am/

You can also find them on the Bible Study Media App's Digital Library page in your App Store on your mobile device or on the Bible Study Media App/Channel on Apple TV or Roku.

The Gathering of the Manna by James Tissot

Video Notes

The Lord's deliverance leads to a process. Miraculously, the Lord parted the waters so that the Israelites could pass through the sea as if walking on dry ground. The Israelites rejoiced at the work of the Lord and celebrated with song, dance, and worship. Their physical bondage was broken! What we learn from their story is that physical healing does not immediately translate to emotional and spiritual healing. The day of deliverance commences the lifelong journey of healing.

Healing involves a process of detachment. It took forty days to get Israel out of Egypt but forty years to get Egypt out of the Israelites. Their journey through the wilderness would serve to heal the Israelites of their idolatry and ungodly attachments. The Israelites would longingly look back to the bondage of Egypt, thinking of the delicacies and security. In the pagan land of Egypt, they had been exposed to the worship of many gods. Now, they must learn to trust in the one true God and to rely on him alone.

Ultimate healing comes through trust and obedience. God provided tests designed to teach Israel to depend on Yahweh for physical health, emotional health, spiritual health, and relational health. Through the Lord's commandments, he protected the people and led them to life.

As you choose to obey the Lord and align your life with him, you will experience the blessings of the Lord, the abundant life he has planned for you, and the promised ultimate healing of eternal life with him. As the beloved hymn states, "Trust and obey."

SHEMA: HEARING GOD'S COVENANT WORD

Read Exodus 16:1-21: Manna in the Wilderness

3. In Exodus 16:3, what do you observe about the Israelites' co-dependence with Egypt? Why was it so hard for them to detach from their former bondage?

4. Healing teaches us to trust, know, and walk with God for continued healing. Why do you think God would not allow the "bread from the Lord" to be collected and saved (16:19-21) beyond the day's need (except for the Sabbath day)?

5. They have experienced God's mighty hand guiding them, providing quail and manna for them, and defending them from their enemies. Why does it seem so hard for the people of Israel to trust and obey God?

TABERNACLE: JOURNEYING WITH GLORY

6. "You yourselves have seen what I did to the Egyptians, and how I bore you on eagles' wings and brought you to myself. Now therefore, if you will indeed obey my voice and keep my covenant, you shall be my treasured possession among all peoples, for all the earth is mine; and you shall be to me a kingdom of priests and a holy nation" (Exodus 19:4-6). Do you see yourself as God's treasured possession? What does it mean that the Lord bore his people on eagles' wings and brought them to himself? How has he done that for you?

7. The Lord says that the nation of Israel will be a kingdom of priests and a holy nation. What does it mean to be holy (sanctified)? How do holiness, healing, and obedience come together in the church today (See 1 Peter 2:9-12)?

8. John 10:10 states, "The thief comes only to steal, kill, and destroy, but I have come that they may have life and have it abundantly." How do you see trust and obedience leading to this abundant life?

9. When the Lord declares that he is the one who heals his people, he looks forward to the coming of Christ and the physical, spiritual, and mental healings Jesus would perform. The Lord looks to heal the whole person. How would you purpose to seek the Lord's healing in your life this week?

PRAYER REQUESTS

You may want to share prayer requests with one another. There's a Prayer & Praise Journal found on p. 64 where you can keep track of your group's requests. Have someone close in prayer or pray together as a group.

CLOSING PRAYER

Week 5 — THE GOD WHO SPEAKS TO HIS PEOPLE
Exodus 20:1-24:18

QUESTION
How did Yahweh reveal his will to his people, Israel? Does God still speak to us today?

KEY VERSE
"And God spoke all these words, saying, 'I am the Lord your God, who brought you out of the land of Egypt, out of the house of slavery. You shall have no other gods before me.'"
— Exodus 20:1-3

SESSION INTRODUCTION

Intimate communication is central to the special relationship that Yahweh has with his people, Israel. The Lord wants his people to know him and to be faithful to his Word. In an awesome scene, the Lord revealed himself to the people of Israel on the holy mountain called Sinai. Earlier in the Exodus, God spoke to Moses. Here, he is addressing his people.

At the heart of God's self-disclosure are ten "words," or commandments, that define the covenant boundaries of the relationship Israel would have with him and with one another. These provided the foundational framework for the 613 laws found in the five books of Moses: Genesis, Exodus, Leviticus, Numbers, and Deuteronomy.

Jesus is described by writers of the New Testament as the supreme and ultimate Word of God. The writer of Hebrews opens his letter with these words: *"Long ago, at many times and in many ways, God spoke to our fathers by the prophets, but in these last days he has spoken to us by his Son..."* (Hebrews 1:1-2a).

READING PLAN: WEEK FIVE

DAY 29	EXODUS 20:1-26
DAY 30	EXODUS 21:1-32
DAY 31	EXODUS 21:33-22:15
DAY 32	EXODUS 22:16-23:9
DAY 33	EXODUS 23:10-19
DAY 34	EXODUS 23:20-33
DAY 35	EXODUS 24:1-18

EXODUS: LEAVING EGYPT

Opening Prayer

Heavenly Father, you are a God who speaks to his people. In times past, you have spoken through angels and prophets, but in these last days you have spoken through your Son. Open our ears and hearts to know your Word and your will for our lives. In Jesus Christ's name we pray, Amen.

Getting Started

1. Do you think God still speaks to his people today?

2. What is the dominant voice governing our culture today? Do you think people are open to listening to God?

SINAI: MEETING AT THE MOUNTAIN

Watch the Video

The video teaching resources for The Great "I AM": A Study of the Book of Exodus may be found on the web at: biblestudymedia.com/pages/the-great-i-am/

You can also find them on the Bible Study Media App's Digital Library page in your App Store on your mobile device or on the Bible Study Media App/Channel on Apple TV or Roku.

Moses on Mount Sinai by Daniele da Volterra

Video Notes

Moses is a mediator. The voice of the Lord is powerful and awesome. As the people approached the holy mountain of Sinai, they were overcome with fear as they beheld God's glory and heard his thunderous voice. Out of their fear, they commissioned Moses to be a mediator of God's word to them. The story of Mount Sinai would stand as a perpetual reminder that the Law of Moses was divinely inspired and authoritative.

Yahweh is a jealous God. At the heart of the commands of God is a singular commitment to be exclusive and absolute in fidelity to Yahweh alone. Worship and love of other deities would not be tolerated. Think about the covenant between Yahweh and Israel like a marriage; idolatry is the religious equivalent of adultery. To state it positively, Jesus called this the Great Commandment: "Love the Lord your God with all your heart and with all your soul and with all your mind and with all your strength" (Deuteronomy 6:5 and Mark 12:30).

Jesus is the supreme Word of God. Jesus is the Word made flesh. The New Testament describes him as the ultimate and final revelation of God. On the Mountain of Transfiguration, the apostles, like Moses and the prophet Elijah, are given a glimpse of the Shekinah Glory of God and hear the thunderous voice of the Father, "This is my Son... Listen to him" (Matthew 17:5).

Pentecost is a New Sinai. After Jesus' resurrection and ascension, the Word of God is to be written on human hearts. On the festival of the Day of Pentecost, the annual celebration of the giving of the Law at Mount Sinai, the followers of Jesus were empowered from within by the gift of the Holy Spirit. Miraculous speech poured forth from their lips, and they heard the praises of God spoken in the languages of the world.

SHEMA: HEARING GOD'S COVENANT WORD

Read Exodus 20:1-21: The Ten Commandments

3. How do you feel about the idea that Yahweh is a jealous God who wants exclusive worship (20:5) from his people?

4. The Ten Commandments are often summarized into two categories: love of God and love of neighbor. How does the love of neighbor (Commandments 5-10) relate to and flow out of the love of God (Commandments 1-4)?

5. Why did the people need a mediator between them and God (20:18-21)? How does the writer of Hebrews describe Jesus in comparison to Moses and the prophets of old (See Hebrews 1:1-4)?

TABERNACLE: JOURNEYING WITH GLORY

6. Read Jeremiah 31:31-33. How is the promised new covenant going to differ from the covenant and commandments offered by Moses?

7. In your walk with God, have you had any Mount Sinai moments where you dramatically heard God speaking to you?

8. Why is it so hard for us to remain attentive and obedient to the Word of God?

9. What could you do to engage in reflection on the Word of God in the coming week?

PRAYER REQUESTS

You may want to share prayer requests with one another. There's a Prayer & Praise Journal found on p. 64 where you can keep track of your group's requests. Have someone close in prayer or pray together as a group.

CLOSING PRAYER

Week 6 — THE GOD WHO DWELLS WITH HIS PEOPLE
Exodus 25:1-28:43

QUESTION
What is the tent of meeting and what is its significance for the people of God?

KEY VERSE
"And let them make me a sanctuary, that I may dwell in their midst. Exactly as I show you concerning the pattern of the tabernacle, and of all its furniture, so you shall make it."
— Exodus 25:8-9

SESSION INTRODUCTION

The people of Israel were to be a people who themselves mediated the presence of God to the world. The Lord would dwell in the midst of his people. They would set up their camp around a special meeting place called the tabernacle, or tent of meeting.

In Exodus, we find the instructions on how to construct the tabernacle and its furniture. The architectural specifications of the tabernacle were exacting in their precision: the materials to be used, the dimensions, and even the colors. Each piece of furniture had a specific purpose in the worship of Yahweh.

Special craftsmen would use their gifts and talents inspired by God to complete this magnificent structure. God would pour out his Spirit on certain people for specific tasks. The instruction manual on how to use the tabernacle and its various accoutrements would be revealed in the third book of Moses, Leviticus.

The writers of the Gospels would reveal that Jesus' body is the true tabernacle (See John 1:14, 2:21). As God incarnate, Jesus was the tabernacle of God. As he walked the earth with God's glory manifested in his person, and with his ascension to the right hand of the Father, his Holy Spirit fills the Church as a living temple of the Lord where his glory is pleased to dwell.

READING PLAN: WEEK SIX

DAY 36	EXODUS 25:1–22
DAY 37	EXODUS 25:23–40
DAY 38	EXODUS 26:1–14
DAY 39	EXODUS 26:15–37
DAY 40	EXODUS 27:1–21
DAY 41	EXODUS 28:1–21
DAY 42	EXODUS 28:22–43

EXODUS: LEAVING EGYPT

Opening Prayer

Lord God, just as you came and dwelt with the people of Israel, so now you come to dwell within us by your Holy Spirit. Help us to prepare our hearts, our minds, and our lives so that we may be a holy dwelling place for you. May others see your presence in us and be drawn to you. In the name of Jesus Christ, Amen.

Getting Started

1. Where do you experience the presence of God in your life?

2. Have you ever visited the Oval Office of the U.S. president or the throne room of royalty? What was it like?

SINAI: MEETING AT THE MOUNTAIN

Watch the Video

The video teaching resources for The Great "I AM": A Study of the Book of Exodus may be found on the web at: biblestudymedia.com/pages/the-great-i-am/

You can also find them on the Bible Study Media App's Digital Library page in your App Store on your mobile device or on the Bible Study Media App/Channel on Apple TV or Roku.

The Jewish tabernacle and priesthood by George C. Needham in Internet Archive Book Images

Video Notes

God designed the tent of meeting. The structure followed a pattern of a throne room. The writer of Hebrews says that it was a copy of the heavenly throne room of God. The structure had three chambers each appointed with specific furniture. The central and innermost room was the Holy of Holies. This room contained the most important piece of furniture, the Ark of the Covenant.

The furniture had purpose. These items all became the center of Israel's approach to and worship of Yahweh. The Ark of the Covenant with the mercy seat was the footstool of the throne of Yahweh. Only Moses and Aaron could approach the presence of the High King of Heaven in the Most Holy Place. From here, the Lord would speak with them and give commands to his people.

You shall make it. Even the building of this sacred structure would be an act of worship and sacrificial offering. The materials and labor for the construction of the tent of meeting would be entirely provided by the people of God and by their life and labor.

Jesus' body is the tabernacle. With Jesus' resurrection and ascension, the Church becomes the corporate Body of Christ and a new living structure, made not with human hands but out of human beings. The people of God become the dwelling place of God.

SHEMA: HEARING GOD'S COVENANT WORD

Read Exodus 25:1-22: The Sanctuary and the Ark of the Covenant

3. The contributions for the construction of the tabernacle and its furniture would come from the people. Why do you think the Lord said these gifts should come *"from every man whose heart moves him"* (v. 2)?

4. What is the purpose of a sanctuary? Why do you think they had to make it "exactly" (v. 9) as it was shown to Moses (See Hebrews 8:5)?

5. The Ark of the Covenant with the mercy seat formed the central piece of furniture in the Most Holy Place where Moses and Aaron the High Priest would meet with God, hear his voice, and offer blood sacrifice for sin. Read Hebrews 9:11-14. How has Jesus fulfilled the significance and usefulness of the tabernacle and its furniture?

TABERNACLE: JOURNEYING WITH GLORY

6. How important is it that we each contribute our time, tithes, and talents to the worship of God? What happens to the people of God when these things are withheld?

7. Read Ephesians 2:18-22. What do you think Paul means when he says that you are *"being joined together into a holy temple of the Lord"* (v. 21)? What are the implications of this for the unity of the Church and our significance to the people of the world?

8. Have you discerned your spiritual gifts and vocation as a servant of the Lord's sanctuary? Perhaps you may want to encourage other members of your group in what you have seen in them as their spiritual gifts and contribution to the body of Christ.

PRAYER REQUESTS

You may want to share prayer requests with one another. There's a Prayer & Praise Journal found on p. 64 where you can keep track of your group's requests. Have someone close in prayer or pray together as a group.

CLOSING PRAYER

Week 7 — THE GOD WHO SANCTIFIES HIS PEOPLE
Exodus 29:1-32:35

QUESTION
What does it mean to be God's holy people?

KEY VERSE
"And the Lord said to Moses, 'You are to speak to the people of Israel and say, "Above all you shall keep my Sabbaths, for this is a sign between me and you throughout your generations, that you may know that I, the Lord, sanctify you."'" — Exodus 31:12-13

SESSION INTRODUCTION

The Lord has led his people out of the land of Egypt and out of the bondage of slavery. Now he must teach them how to live as his holy people. The Lord set his love upon the nation of Israel. As his chosen people, they are to live differently than the other nations.

As the Lord provides instructions for his tabernacle, the priests, and the sacrificial system, the people will see that there is a cost to holiness. Sin requires costly atonement. If the Lord will come and dwell among his people, they must be prepared. Throughout these chapters, we will learn about the specificity of that preparation and the intentionality of living a holy life.

A holy lifestyle must inform every aspect of their lives – their worship, their diet, their laws, their relationships. The Apostle Peter writes: *"You shall be holy, for I am holy"* (1 Peter 1:16). Just as the nation of Israel was called to live as the Lord's set apart nation, so we as followers of Christ today are called to live holy lives that reflect the glory of God to the world.

READING PLAN: WEEK SEVEN

DAY 43	EXODUS 29:1-21
DAY 44	EXODUS 29:22-46
DAY 45	EXODUS 30:1-21
DAY 46	EXODUS 30:22-38
DAY 47	EXODUS 31:1-18
DAY 48	EXODUS 32:1-20
DAY 49	EXODUS 32:21-35

EXODUS: LEAVING EGYPT

Opening Prayer

Only you, Lord, can cleanse us of our sins. You have called us to live as your set apart people, as people who are distinct from the world. Help us to embrace this call. Help us in our weakness. Create in us a desire for you, for your will, and for your way in our lives. Consecrate us today by your Holy Spirit. In Jesus Christ's name, Amen.

Getting Started

1. What do you think it means to be holy? What about holiness is most challenging to you?

2. How would you characterize a holy person? Who is an example of a holy person for you?

SINAI: MEETING AT THE MOUNTAIN

Watch the Video

The video teaching resources for The Great "I AM": A Study of the Book of Exodus may be found on the web at: biblestudymedia.com/pages/the-great-i-am/

You can also find them on the Bible Study Media App's Digital Library page in your App Store on your mobile device or on the Bible Study Media App/Channel on Apple TV or Roku.

Moses and Joshua bowing before the Ark by James Tissot

Video Notes

Keep the Sabbath. The Sabbath is God's covenant with the nation of Israel. They are to work for six days, but on the seventh day, they are to rest just as the Lord worked for six days in creation and on the seventh day rested. In keeping this covenant, the nation of Israel was reminded that they were the Lord's people. He was the one who rescued them out of the land of Egypt, and he is the one who will sanctify them as his people.

Give a tithe to God. Just as Yahweh is the one who rescued them from slavery, he is also the one who provides for them. We see the water from the rock and the daily provision of manna and quail. Since God is the giver of every good gift, the people are to learn the act of a tithe – the giving back to God from all that he has entrusted to them. All that the Israelites have is a gift from God.

Israel is a holy people and a kingdom of priests. While every other nation surrounding the Israelites served many gods, the nation of Israel was called to worship the one true God—and him alone. They were not to create for themselves any idols. The Lord understood their propensity to worship the work of their hands. He wanted full access to their hearts and to live in a special relationship with them. To do so, they needed to be cleansed of all other forms of worship. The entire nation was set apart as a holy people to mediate God's covenant to the world.

SHEMA: HEARING GOD'S COVENANT WORD

Read Exodus 29:38-46: Consecration

3. If God were to dwell among his people, they must be consecrated and set apart. Why do you think it was required to offer animal sacrifices in order to meet with God?

4. The priests are instructed to make a daily offering of lambs, one lamb offered in the morning and another lamb offered at twilight. What is the significance of this continual offering? Compare these offerings with the offering of Jesus in Hebrews 9:24-26.

5. What do you think it means that the people will be sanctified by God's glory (29:43)? Read Hebrews 10:10. How does Jesus sanctify us today?

TABERNACLE: JOURNEYING WITH GLORY

6. What is the attitude towards sin in our society today? Do you think that we as a church take sin seriously?

7. Discuss the commandment to keep the Sabbath holy. What did that look like for the nation of Israel, and what does that look like for you today? Why do you think the Sabbath holds such importance to God?

8. The gift of the tithe demonstrates that we know that all good things come from the hand of God. Peter calls us to be cheerful givers. What is your heart towards the giving of the tithe (10% of your income)? What has been most challenging for you in tithing, and when have you seen blessings from tithing?

9. In Romans 12, we are called to a new kind of sacrifice. Paul writes, *"I appeal to you therefore, brothers, by the mercies of God, to present your bodies as a living sacrifice, holy and acceptable to God, which is your spiritual worship"* (Romans 12:1). What does it look like to offer yourself, your body as a living sacrifice to God?

PRAYER REQUESTS

You may want to share prayer requests with one another. There's a Prayer & Praise Journal found on p. 64 where you can keep track of your group's requests. Have someone close in prayer or pray together as a group.

CLOSING PRAYER

Week 8

THE GOD WHO LOVES HIS PEOPLE
Exodus 33:1-36:38

QUESTION

How has the Lord's steadfast love been revealed?

KEY VERSE

"The Lord passed before him and proclaimed, 'The Lord, the Lord, a God merciful and gracious, slow to anger, and abounding in steadfast love and faithfulness, keeping steadfast love for thousands, forgiving iniquity and transgression and sin, but who will by no means clear the guilty, visiting the iniquity of the fathers on the children and the children's children, to the third and fourth generation." — Exodus 34:6-7

SESSION INTRODUCTION

While Moses was on the mountain, the Israelites made and then worshipped the golden calf. Just before Moses ascended the mountain, the people had declared whole-heartedly that all God said they would do. How quickly they forgot their promise! Nevertheless, as Moses goes back up the mountain to receive the commandments of the Lord once again, the Lord speaks of his hesed—the Hebrew word for steadfast love.

Graciously, the Lord continues to reveal that steadfast love. When Moses requests to see God's glory, the Lord reveals aspects of his glory: his grace and mercy, he is slow to anger, and he abounds in steadfast love and faithfulness.

In experiencing this love of the Lord, Moses is transformed – just as the nation of Israel will be changed by following the commands of the Lord. The Lord's steadfast love not only transforms his people but also differentiates his people.

READING PLAN: WEEK EIGHT

DAY 50	EXODUS 33:1-33
DAY 51	EXODUS 34:1-20
DAY 52	EXODUS 34:21-38
DAY 53	EXODUS 35:1-19
DAY 54	EXODUS 35:20-35
DAY 55	EXODUS 36:1-19
DAY 56	EXODUS 36:20-38

Opening Prayer

In you alone, O Lord, do we experience the steadfast love of your covenant faithfulness. Open our hearts to receive this perfect love. Cover us in your mercy and grace and teach us how to live as your chosen and beloved children. In the name of our Lord Jesus Christ, Amen.

Getting Started

1. When you think about the nature of God, what attributes first come to your mind?

2. After the golden calf incident, the Lord tells Moses that he will not go among the people anymore. How do you see God's mercy in this?

SINAI: MEETING AT THE MOUNTAIN

Watch the Video

The video teaching resources for The Great "I AM": A Study of the Book of Exodus may be found on the web at: biblestudymedia.com/pages/the-great-i-am/

You can also find them on the Bible Study Media App's Digital Library page in your App Store on your mobile device or on the Bible Study Media App/Channel on Apple TV or Roku.

Adoration of the Golden Calf by Andrea di Lione

Video Notes

God reveals his attributes. The visible manifestation of the attributes of God comes through the revelation of his glory. Moses asks to see the Lord's glory. While Moses wanted to see the Lord; the Lord knew Moses needed to understand his character, his attributes, and his covenantal love for the people. God gave Moses what he needed instead of what he wanted.

God shows steadfast love. The love of the Lord leads to assurance. Though his people have sinned grievously, the Lord's love remains upon them. They are still his people, and they still have all the benefits of the covenant. The Lord's love for Israel is not based on their behavior but upon his covenantal promises to the patriarchs.

God's glory is reflected on Moses. The presence of the Lord transformed Moses. When he came down from the mountain, his face shone with the reflected glory of God. No other god impacted his followers the way Yahweh did. No other person in history has been said to reflect the glory of his God but Moses.

SHEMA: HEARING GOD'S COVENANT WORD

Read Exodus 33:12-23: Moses' Intercession

3. In this passage of Scripture, what do you think is meant by the word "glory"?

4. Moses tells the Lord that it is his presence that sets the nation of Israel apart from the other nations. The Lord remains with his people. His presence assures them of his love. We, too, have the presence of God. How do you experience the love of God through his presence?

5. Read Exodus 34:6-7. Why do you think the Lord designates the number of generations to whom he will keep his promises versus the number to whom he will execute justice? What does the difference between these multigenerational commitments say about the nature and character of Yahweh?

6. When Moses asked to see God's glory, the Lord told Moses that he would make all his goodness pass before him. What was the manifestation of God's goodness? How do you think that manifestation would minister to Moses?

TABERNACLE: JOURNEYING WITH GLORY

7. *"May the Lord direct your hearts to the love of God and to the steadfastness of Christ"* (2 Thessalonians 3:5). How does Jesus' death and resurrection assure you of God's steadfast love?

8. Our lives are to reflect God's glory to this dark world. In Matthew 5, we are told to be salt and light. How can we live as salt and light?

9. Moses moved from being an insecure and fearful leader to a bold leader of the Israelite nation. Read Acts 4:8-13. Here we see the disciples transformed into bold witnesses for Christ. What made the difference for these men? How can you become this kind of bold leader?

10. Moses was transformed by beholding God's glory. Each time he met with the Lord, his face shone. Read 2 Corinthians 3:17-18, and discuss how you are transformed by meeting with the living God.

PRAYER REQUESTS

You may want to share prayer requests with one another. There's a Prayer & Praise Journal found on p. 64 where you can keep track of your group's requests. Have someone close in prayer or pray together as a group.

CLOSING PRAYER

Week 9 — THE GOD WHO GUIDES HIS PEOPLE
Exodus 37:1-40:38

QUESTION
How does God guide his people?

KEY VERSE
"Throughout all their journeys, whenever the cloud was taken up from over the tabernacle, the people of Israel would set out. But if the cloud was not taken up, then they did not set out till the day that it was taken up." — Exodus 40:36-37

SESSION INTRODUCTION

The Lord has rescued the nation of Israel from the bondage of Egypt. They have been delivered, redeemed, and healed. Now we see the Lord guiding his people by the cloud. During the day, the cloud provides covering for the people. At night, it provides light.

Thus, the Lord directs his people with his presence. They go when he moves, and they stay when he stays. The people surrender their plans and their timing to follow the Lord.

The Lord still wants to direct his people. Often, we miss out on his plans because we struggle to wait on his guidance and his timing. While we don't have the glory cloud, we have God's presence dwelling within us. He longs to reveal his plans, his purposes, and his timing. Will we have eyes to see him, ears to hear him, and a heart ready to obey?

READING PLAN: WEEK NINE

DAY 57	EXODUS 37:1-24
DAY 58	EXODUS 37:25-38:8
DAY 59	EXODUS 38:9-31
DAY 60	EXODUS 39:1-21
DAY 61	EXODUS 39:22-43
DAY 62	EXODUS 40:1-19
DAY 63	EXODUS 40:20-38

Opening Prayer

Father, just as you led the nation of Israel out of Egypt and through the wilderness, so we ask that you guide us today. Empower us through your Holy Spirit to discern what your good, pleasing, and perfect will is for our lives. In Jesus Christ's name, Amen.

Getting Started

1. How do you experience the guidance of the Lord?

2. The Lord dwelt with the nation of Israel in the tabernacle. How does he dwell with his people today?

SINAI: MEETING AT THE MOUNTAIN

Watch the Video

The video teaching resources for The Great "I AM": A Study of the Book of Exodus may be found on the web at: biblestudymedia.com/pages/the-great-i-am/

You can also find them on the Bible Study Media App's Digital Library page in your App Store on your mobile device or on the Bible Study Media App/Channel on Apple TV or Roku.

Joshua passing the River Jordan with the Ark of the Covenant by Benjamin West

Video Notes

God guides us through his indwelling presence. The glory of God was made manifest within the camp of Israel through the pillar of cloud and fire. God directed as to when to move and when to remain and wait. In the same way, God's Holy Spirit dwells within us to guide and direct us.

We walk with the Lord. The response of the people of God is to walk with God when he moves. We are to observe where God is acting in power and join him in the march and in the battle.

We wait on the Lord. There are other times when God's people are called to wait on the Lord for direction. During these times of patient endurance, the Lord is often teaching his people lessons in trust and provision.

We wrestle with the Lord. The Lord never discounts the pleas, prayers, and petitions of his people. The name Israel means "wrestles with God." He wants us to wrestle with his will in a dynamic relationship of back and forth.

SHEMA: HEARING GOD'S COVENANT WORD

Read Exodus 40:16-38: The Tabernacle and the Glory of the Lord

3. Moses was faithful to obey all that the Lord commanded. Because of this faithfulness, God's glory filled the tabernacle. Imagine what that must have been like for Moses and the Israelites. How do we see this kind of glory today?

4. Now imagine not being among the Israelites but seeing them pass through the land, following a cloud, and carrying this tabernacle. What do you think your impressions would be?

5. What was the role of Aaron and his sons in the tabernacle? How did they serve the nation of Israel?

TABERNACLE: JOURNEYING WITH GLORY

6. "And the Word became flesh and dwelt among us, and we have seen his glory, glory as of the only Son from the Father, full of grace and truth" (John 1:14). In this verse, "dwelt" is the same word that was used for "tabernacle" in Exodus. What does it mean that Jesus came to tabernacle/dwell with his people?

7. It is hard to surrender our agendas and our timing in order to surrender to God's plans and God's timing. The nation of Israel knew when to move and when to wait. How do you discern this guidance of the Lord?

8. Where do you see Jesus moving and directing in our day and what steps could you take to go and join him?

PRAYER REQUESTS

You may want to share prayer requests with one another. There's a Prayer & Praise Journal found on p. 64 where you can keep track of your group's requests. Have someone close in prayer or pray together as a group.

CLOSING PRAYER

appendices

FREQUENTLY ASKED QUESTIONS

What do we do on the first night of our group?
Have a party! A "get to know you" coffee, dinner, or dessert is a great way to launch a new study. You may want to review the Small Group Covenant (page 62) and share the names of a few friends you can invite to join you. But most importantly, have fun before your study time begins.

Where do we find new member for our group?
Finding members can be troubling, especially for new groups that have only a few people or for existing groups that lose a few people along the way. We encourage you to pray with your group and then brainstorm a list of people from work, church, your neighborhood, your children's school, family, the gym, and so forth. Use the five circles to identify potential group members with whom you would like to build a spiritual friendship. Have each group member invite several of the people on his or her list.

No matter how you find members, it's vital that you stay on the lookout for new people to join your group. All groups tend to go through healthy attrition—the result of moves, sending out new leaders, ministry opportunities, and so forth—and if the group gets too small, it could be at risk of ending. If you and your group stay open to ideas, you'll be amazed at the people God sends your way. The next person just might become a friend for life. You never know!

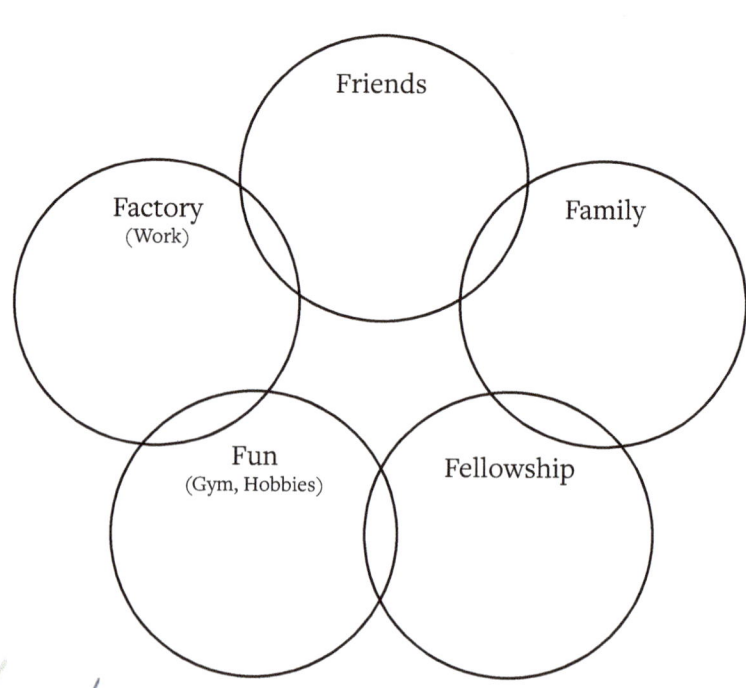

How long will this group meet?
Most groups meet weekly for at least their first 6 weeks, but every other week can work as well. We strongly recommend that the group meet for the first 6 months on a weekly basis if at all possible. This allows for continuity and, if people miss a meeting, they aren't gone for a whole month.

At the end of this study, each group member may decide if he or she wants to continue on for another study. Some groups launch relationships for years to come, and others are stepping-stones into another group experience. Either way, enjoy the journey.

Can we do this study on our own?
Absolutely! This may sound crazy, but one of the best ways to do this study is not with a full house but with a few friends. You may choose to gather with just one or two friends who would enjoy some relational time (perhaps going to the movies or having a quiet dinner) and then walking through this study. Jesus will be with you even if there are only two of you (Matthew 18:20).

What if this group is not working for us?
You're not alone! This could be the result of a personality conflict, life stage difference, geographical distance, level of spiritual maturity, or any number of things. Relax. Pray for God's direction, and at the end of this study, decide whether to continue with this group or find another. You don't typically buy the first car you test drive or marry the first person you date, and the same goes with a group. However, don't bail out before the 9 weeks are up— God might have something to teach you. Also, don't run from conflict or prejudge people before you have given them a chance. God is still working in your life, too!

Who is the leader?
Most groups have an official leader. But ideally, the group will mature and members will rotate the leadership of meetings. We have discovered that healthy groups rotate hosts/leaders and homes on a regular basis. This model ensures that all members grow, make their unique contribution, and develop their gifts. This study guide and the Holy Spirit can keep things on track even when you rotate leaders. Christ has promised to be in your midst as you gather. Ultimately, God is your leader each step of the way.

How do we handle the childcare needs in our group?
Very carefully. This can be a sensitive issue. We suggest that you empower the group to openly brainstorm solutions. You may try one option that works for a while and then adjust over time. Our favorite approach is for adults to meet in the living room or dining room and to share the cost of a babysitter (or two) who can watch the children in a different part of the house. This way, parents don't have to be away from their children all evening when their children are too young to be left at home. A second option is to use one home for the children and a second home (close by or a phone call away) for the adults. A third idea is to rotate the responsibility of providing a lesson or care for the children either in the same home or in another home nearby. This can be an incredible blessing for young ones. Finally, the most common solution is to decide that you need to have a night to invest in your spiritual lives individually or as a couple and to make your own arrangements for childcare. No matter what decision the group makes, the best approach is to dialogue openly about both the need and the solution.

small group covenant

OUR PURPOSE
To provide a predictable environment where participants experience authentic Christian community to grow spiritually.

GROUP ATTENDANCE
To give priority to the group meeting. We will call or email if we will be late or absent. (Completing the Group Calendar on p. 63 will minimize this issue.)

SAFE ENVIRONMENT
To help create a safe place where people can be heard and feel loved. (Please, no quick answers, snap judgments, or simple fixes.)

RESPECT DIFFERENCES
To be gentle and gracious with different spiritual maturity levels, personal opinions, temperaments, or "imperfections" in fellow group members. We are all works in progress.

CONFIDENTIALITY
To keep anything shared strictly confidential and within the group, and to avoid sharing improper information about those outside the group.

ENCOURAGEMENT FOR GROWTH
To be not just takers, but givers of life. We want to spiritually multiply our lives by serving others with our God-given gifts.

SHARED OWNERSHIP
To remember that every member is a minister and to ensure that each attender will share a small team role or responsibility over time.

ROTATING HOSTS, FACILITATORS, AND HOMES
To encourage different people to host the group in their homes and to rotate the responsibility of facilitating each meeting. (See the Group Calendar on p.63)

group calendar

Date	Session	Host Home	Snacks	Facilitator
	1			
	2			
	3			
	4			
	5			
	6			
	7			
	8			
	9			

prayer and praise journal

Session 1

_____
_____
_____
_____

Session 2

_____
_____
_____
_____

Session 3

_____
_____
_____
_____

Session 4

_____
_____
_____
_____

Session 5

_____

Session 6

_____

Session 7

_____

Session 8

_____

Session 9

_____

small group roster

Name	Email	Cell Phone

small group leader helps

Hosting an Open House
If you're starting a new group, try planning an Open House before your first formal group meeting. Even if you have only two to four core members, it's a great way to break the ice and prayerfully consider who else might be open to joining you over the next few weeks. You can also use this kick-off meeting to hand out books, spend some time getting to know each other, discuss each person's expectations for the group, and briefly pray for each other. A simple meal or good dessert always makes a kick-off meeting more fun. After people introduce themselves and share how they ended up at the meeting (you can play a game to see who has the wildest story!), have everyone respond to a few icebreaker questions, such as:

- What is your favorite family vacation?
- What is one thing you love about your church/our community?
- What are two things about your life growing up that most people here don't know?

Next, ask everyone to tell what they hope to get out of the study. You might want to review the Small Group Covenant on p. 62 and discuss each person's expectations and priorities. Finally, set an open chair (maybe two) in the center of your group and explain that it represents someone who would enjoy or benefit from this group who isn't here yet.

Ask people to pray about inviting someone to join the group over the next few weeks. Hand out postcards and have everyone write an invitation or two. Don't worry about having too many people. You can always have one discussion circle in the living room and another in the dining room after you watch the lesson. Each group could then report prayer requests and progress at the end of the session.

You can skip this kick-off meeting if your time is limited, but you'll experience a huge benefit if you take the time to connect with one another in this way.

Leading for the First Time
Seven common leadership experiences. Welcome to life out in front!

- **Sweaty palms are a healthy sign.** The Bible says God is gracious to the humble. Remember who is in control; the time to worry is when you're not worried. Those who are soft in heart (and sweaty-palmed) are those whom God is sure to speak through.

- **Seek support.** Ask your leader, co-leader, or a close friend to pray for you and prepare with you before the session. Walking through the study will help you anticipate potentially difficult questions and discussion topics.

- **Bring your uniqueness to the study.** Lean into who you are and how God wants you to lead the study uniquely.

- **Prepare. Prepare. Prepare.** Go through the session, and read the section of Scripture. If you are using the video, listen to the teaching segment. Consider writing in a journal or praying through the day to prepare yourself for what God wants to do. Don't wait until the last minute to prepare.

- **Ask for feedback so you can grow.** Perhaps in an email or on index cards handed out at the study, have everyone write down three things you did well and one thing you could improve on. Don't get defensive. Instead, show an openness to learn and grow.

- **Share with your group what God is doing in your heart.** God is searching for those whose hearts are fully his. Share your trials and victories. We promise that people will relate.

- **Prayerfully consider whom you would like to pass the baton to next week.** It's only fair. God is ready for the next member of your group to go on the faith journey you just traveled. Make it fun, and expect God to do the rest.

Leadership Training 101

Congratulations! You have responded to the call to help shepherd Jesus' flock. Few other tasks in the family of God surpass the contribution you will be making. As you prepare to lead, whether for one session or the entire series, here are a few thoughts to keep in mind. We encourage you to read and review these with each new discussion leader before they lead.

1. Remember, you are not alone. God knows everything about you, and he knew you would be asked to lead this group. It is common for all good leaders to feel they are not ready to lead. Moses, Solomon, Jeremiah, and Timothy were all reluctant to lead. God promises, "*Never will I leave you; never will I forsake you*" (Hebrews 13:5). Whether you are leading for one evening, several weeks, or a lifetime, you will be blessed as you serve.

2. Don't try to do it alone. Pray right now for God to help you build a healthy leadership team. If you can enlist a co-leader to help you lead the group, you will find your experience much richer. This is your chance to involve as many people as possible in building a healthy group. All you have to do is call and ask people to help. You'll probably be surprised at the response.

3. Just be yourself. If you won't be you, who will? God wants you to use your unique gifts and temperament. Don't try to do things exactly like another leader; do them in a way that fits you! Just admit it when you don't have an answer and apologize when you make a mistake. Your group will love you for it, and you'll sleep better at night!

4. Prepare for your meeting ahead of time. Review the session and write down your responses to each question. Pay special attention to exercises that ask group members to do something other than engage in discussion, like take an action. These exercises will help your group live what the Bible teaches, not just talk about it.

5. Pray for your group members by name. Before you begin your session, go around the room in your mind and pray for each member. Ask God to use your time together to touch every person's heart uniquely. Expect God to lead you to whomever he wants you to encourage or challenge in a special way. If you listen, God will surely lead!

6. When you ask a question, be patient. Someone will eventually respond. Sometimes people need a moment or two of silence to think about the question. Keep in mind, if silence doesn't bother you, it won't bother anyone else. After someone responds, affirm the response with a simple "thanks" or "good job." Then ask, "How about somebody else?" or "Would someone who hasn't shared like to add anything?" Be sensitive to new people or members who aren't ready to say, pray, or do anything. If you give them a safe setting, they will blossom over time.

7. Provide transitions between questions. Always read aloud the transitional paragraphs and questions when guiding the discussion. Ask the group if anyone would like to read the paragraphs or Bible passages. Don't call on anyone, but ask for volunteers; be patient until someone begins. Be sure to thank the people who read aloud.

8. Break up into small groups each week, or a larger group won't stay. If your group has a lot of people, we strongly encourage you to have the group sometimes gather in discussion circles of three or four people during the Renew the Covenant sections. With a greater opportunity to talk in small circles, people will connect more with the study, apply more quickly what they're learning, and ultimately get more out of it. A small circle encourages a quiet person to participate and can minimize the effect of a more dominant or vocal member. It can also help people feel more loved in your group.

When you gather again at the end of the section, you can have one person summarize the highlights from each circle. Small circles are also helpful during prayer time. People uncomfortable with praying aloud will feel more comfortable trying it with just two or three others.

Also, prayer requests won't take as much time, so circles will have more time to pray. When you gather back with the whole group, you can have one person from each circle briefly update everyone on the prayer requests. People are more willing to break into small circles to pray if they know the whole group will hear all the prayer requests.

9. Rotate facilitators weekly. At the end of each meeting, ask the group who should lead the following week. Let the group help select your weekly facilitator. You may be perfectly capable of leading each time, but you will help others grow in their faith and gifts if you give them opportunities to lead. You can use the Small Group Calendar (p. 137) to fill in the names of the different leaders for all the meetings if you prefer.

10. One final challenge (for new or first-time leaders): Before your first opportunity to lead, look up each of the five passages listed below. Read each as a devotional exercise to help equip yourself with a shepherd's heart. Trust us on this one. If you do this, you will be more than ready to lead your first meeting.

Matthew 9:36
1 Peter 5:2-4
Psalm 23
Ezekiel 34:11-16
1 Thessalonians 2:7-8, 11-2

notes

notes

notes

www.ingramcontent.com/pod-product-compliance
Lightning Source LLC
Chambersburg PA
CBHW061804070526
44586CB00023B/2713